MW00985396

Becoming a
21st-Century Church

Becoming a 21st-Century Church

A Transformational Manual

J. FRED LEHR

WIPF & STOCK · Eugene, Oregon

BECOMING A 21ST-CENTURY CHURCH
A Transformational Manual

Copyright © 2017 J. Fred Lehr. All rights reserved. Except for brief quotations in critical publications or reviews, no part of this book may be reproduced in any manner without prior written permission from the publisher. Write: Permissions, Wipf and Stock Publishers, 199 W. 8th Ave., Suite 3, Eugene, OR 97401.

Wipf & Stock
An Imprint of Wipf and Stock Publishers
199 W. 8th Ave., Suite 3
Eugene, OR 97401

www.wipfandstock.com

PAPERBACK ISBN: 978-1-5326-3541-0
HARDCOVER ISBN: 978-1-5326-3543-4
EBOOK ISBN: 978-1-5326-3542-7

Manufactured in the U.S.A.   AUGUST 11, 2017

I want to dedicate this transformational manual to all whom I love:

- The Blessed Trinity and God's Holy Church

- My dear wife, Janet; my wonderful children, Jason and Rayanne; and my whole extended family—all the way to my little great-granddaughter, Katherine

- Those committed, brave and eager church leaders, professional and lay, who dare, who risk, who embrace the adventure to faithfully become a twenty-first-century church and face the pushback this journey often elicits

- My friends and colleagues who have encouraged me and supported me in this effort, especially my bishop, William Gohl

- And even those who resist or even oppose this movement to become a twenty-first-century church for whatever reasons—or who are at least in denial. I love them because we are all God's children and are always worthy of love.

Contents

Introduction

What Does It Mean to Be a 21st-Century Church?

IN ORDER TO ANSWER that, I have researched a number of writers and opinions in order to form my own stance on this matter. This manual is my attempt to define what is happening as the church evolves in these days and years and how we can successfully adapt to this change. Failure to adapt can mean the end of the church.

Christianity is always just one generation from extinction. Let me repeat that—Christianity is always just one generation from extinction. Do I believe for a minute that God would allow the church to become extinct? No, not at all.

But in a number of ways, I do believe the current church is not fully an ally in this evolutionary process but rather an impediment. We are not "with the program." In fact, far too many are not even aware of "the program" or are dramatically resistant. In some critical ways, the church is its own worst enemy.

What is this twenty-first-century church?

The primary person to provide some definition is Phyllis Tickle. Her initial work to define this is her book *The Great Emergence: How Christianity Is Changing and Why* (Baker, 2012). This is followed by a more helpful discourse, *Emergence Christianity: What It Is, Where It Is Going, and Why It Matters* (Baker, 2012).

Her theory is that Christianity goes through a major cultural shift every five hundred years. From first generation Christianity—five hundred years later = Monastic Movement—five hundred years later = consolidation of the authority of Rome—five hundred years later = the Reformation—and now—the twenty-first-century church, or as she calls it, the emergent church.

Other authors in this field are people like Brian McLaren (*Generous Orthodoxy*, Zondervon, 2004; *Everything Must Change: Jesus, Global Crisis, and a Revolution of Hope*, Thomas Nelson, 2007); Shane Claiborne (*The Irresistible Revolution: Living as an Ordinary Radical*, Zondervon, 2006) and Claiborne with Jonathan Wilson-Hartgrove (*Becoming the Answer to Our Prayers*, Inter-Varsity, 2008) and also Dan Kimball (*They Like Jesus but Not the Church: Insights from Emerging Generations*, Zondervon, 2007).

Kimball particularly studied young adults and asked them why they no longer go to church. He discovered this list of issues today's young adults have with the church:

- The church is an organized religion with a political agenda
- The church is judgmental and negative
- The church is dominated by males and oppresses females
- The church is homophobic
- The church arrogantly claims all other religions are wrong
- The church is full of fundamentalists who take the whole Bible literally.

Already we see some of our agenda mapped out for us.

If we hope, if we intend, to reach this new twenty-first-century church we are going to have to address these issues and much more.

In addition to Phyllis Tickle's calling the twenty-first-century church the emergent church, some are calling it the postmodern church. And in truth, it is far more than merely for the twenty-first century.

I believe Tickle has it correct. We are now in a new era of the church that is only beginning to take form. It will take a good century to become fully configured. So to call it the twenty-first-century church is simply to say that we need to adapt to where it is now assuming that further adaptations will be required as this new church takes shape.

Additional authors to consider are John Caputo (*Hoping Against Hope: Confessions of a Postmodern Pilgrim*, Fortress, 2015); and someone I highly respect who speaks on a different perspective but has an important contribution is Peter Steinke (*A Door Set Open: Grounding Change in Mission and Hope*, Rowman & Littlefield, 2010). And my own effort to help the church and its clergy to be healthy (*Clergy Burnout: Recovering from the 70-Hour Work Week and Other Self-Defeating Practices*, Augsburg, 2006).

So I have done some significant research in this field, read many articles in addition to these authors, and had countless conversations with colleagues and young adults.

This volume is my attempt to define what we are facing and to provide some practical suggestions how we can make the successful and appropriate adaptations so that the church can thrive in this new era just unfolding around us.

No one asked us if we wanted an evolution in the church to take place. We didn't get to vote on it. It is happening whether we like it or not.

And failure to adjust may mean that congregations will continue to decline and close. As of now, 80 percent of the congregations in most mainline Christian denominations are either stagnant or dying. Eighty percent!

Again, we didn't get to vote on this. It *is* happening. How will we adapt?

Chapter One

What Defines
the 21st-Century Church?

PHYLLIS TICKLE STATES THAT Christianity evolves every five hundred years.

I want to focus most on the most recent evolutions.

The year AD 1,000 gave us the consolidation of the authority of Rome.

Christianity had been spreading throughout the Mediterranean and Middle Eastern regions. It was very localized with each area doing its own things. Opinions and beliefs widely varied. Worship was not at all consistent from place to place.

Who is this Jesus? Human? Divine?

What is the nature of the church?

What are the sacraments? How many? What is the meaning of Holy Communion?

Where does the Holy Trinity factor into this?

Who is the Holy Spirit?

And on and on . . .

The church began to identify the need for some central authority for the sake of orthodoxy, accountability, and just good order. In order to accomplish that, the authority of Rome and the Vatican evolved.

Rome was the center of it all and dictated orthodoxy, controlled authority, and insisted on accountability. It became all about Rome.

The authority of the church was Rome. Rome dictated, the church obeyed.

The character of the church was controlled and defined by Rome. Rome said what the church is and should be.

The power within the church was all about Rome. All power came from Rome and without the consent of Rome there was no power or authority.

Worship, being so controlled by Rome and in a language the common people did not know or speak, became a spectator event. One reason for the bells in worship is so the congregation could know what was happening and what they were supposed to do. The drama of the liturgy, likewise, gave the worshippers a clue what was happening.

The nature of the church was totally controlled by Rome. Nothing was to happen without Rome giving its blessings and consent.

The role of the clergy was to be obedient to Rome. The priest was the servant of Rome and bowed to its authority.

Obedience in the church meant loyalty and allegiance to Rome. The idea of any contradiction with Rome was never allowed.

Opportunity for change in the church was nonexistent. It just could not happen without the agreement of Rome. Rome was in complete control.

Flexibility was likewise extremely limited or nonexistent.

Empowering of the individual within the church also did not exist. All was under the dictates of Rome. The people were to merely follow the wisdom and direction of Rome.

The nature of the faith was also under the dominance of Rome. No one dared dream of the faith from their own perspective. Rome knew best. All would bow to the teachings and knowledge of Rome.

Religious formation was also under the oversight of Rome. Rome provided the means and the methods to grow one's faith even as it decided what that faith should be. Naught without Rome.

Organization within the church was under the tight control of Rome. In the face of the many varied versions of the church that had emerged, Rome took control and organized one central and authoritative system to be obeyed.

Therefore the purpose of the church was to glorify God through Rome. Rome knew best. Do it the way Rome provides.

The focus of the church was on a strict doctrine provided by Rome. To teach or practice otherwise was heresy. And heresy could be punished by death.

The structure of the church was bound and controlled by Rome. Nothing existed without Rome's consent.

And orthodoxy (right belief) was tightly defined by Rome.

All of this was allowed in order to provide a consistent and orderly church in response to the disorder that had developed during the early years. In the face of a chaotic church, one that had discipline and order was preferred.

Thus Rome became the center and the authority of the church for some understandable reasons.

And as the saying goes, "Power corrupts and absolute power corrupts absolutely."

What evolved as a helpful means to address chaos eventually became too dominant and squelched the "human spirit." Freedom within the church failed to exist. Clergy and laity alike became the servants of Rome. It went too far.

So, five hundred years later, around 1500, gave birth to the Reformation.

Actually the Reformation had its roots earlier. John Hus was a martyr one hundred years before Martin Luther showed up.

With the Reformation, the authority of the church made a major shift. From Rome, the authority of the Protestant Church became the Holy Scriptures. One of the battle cries of the Reformation was "sola Scriptura," by Scripture alone!

Now the authority of the church became the Holy Scriptures. The Bible became both the rule book and the manual for the church. It was the Bible that dictated and offered control.

Faithfulness to the Bible was the key determining factor.

So the character of the church was to be found in the Scriptures. Whatever the book said, that's what the church should be.

The power within the church now emanated from the Scriptures. Those who followed "the book" were the ones doing it right. Those who strayed from "the book" were getting it wrong.

Worship still remained mostly spectator (the Pastor does the "hocus pocus" while the parishioners passively watched), but not as much as under Rome. Worshippers were given more to do within the worship experience. And the language of worship became the language of the people. It was not fully their worship as yet, but they were allowed a greater role.

The nature of the church was dictated by the Bible. It was determined by the "rule book" and "manual" that Scripture became to be.

The role of the clergy was to be the ones who knew and fully comprehended all that was in "the book." They were the experts that the laity could turn to for learning. The clergy were to be the learned ones who taught everyone else. They were the "resident theologians" far more than the poor, uneducated laity.

Obedience in the church is now obedience to the Scriptures. As rule book and manual, the Bible was in control now. One's duty was to be faithful to "the book."

Opportunity for change was restricted to the boundaries of the book. As long as it was approved by the Bible, it was okay. Anything not allowed by a strict understanding of the Bible was suspect.

In the same way, flexibility was minimal. If it was not authorized by the book, forget it. It wasn't going to happen.

Even so the empowering of the individual to come to their own conclusions and reach their own understandings was frowned upon. Stick to the book and you won't go wrong. "Trust and obey for there's no other way . . . ," the hymn explained.

The nature of the faith was similarly under the control of the book. One key activity of the church was didactic—teach what is in the book. And in some denominations, the confirmation process merely involved another book, the Catechism.

Knowledge in the church was reflected in how many Bible verses one could memorize. And a hallmark of success in the church was a vast knowledge of Scripture.

Religious formation was defined as learning the book. How well versed was one in all its contents and mandates?

The church was then organized around the book. How faithful to Scripture was the order of the church? Dare to drift and terrible things would happen.

The book provided structure and order.

The purpose of the church was to assist the worshipper to achieve salvation in keeping with the book. The way to heaven was only through the teachings of the book. Learn the book!

The focus of the church was all about the Bible. Readings of the Bible at worship. Preaching on the contents of the Bible. Teaching the Bible in Sunday School. And recruiting children and enlightening them in the summer at Vacation Bible School. It is all about the Bible.

So the church became an institution that was centered and organized around the Bible and for the primary purpose of teaching and preaching the Bible. So much so that eventually, as scriptural criticism began to surface, "institutional survival" became a holy endeavor lest the Bible fall in its importance.

And orthodoxy is all about the Scriptures.

Let me be clear, this *sola Scriptura* church was just the right thing for that point in time. Luther and the Reformers did not make a mistake. They were enlightened by the Holy Spirit to lead the church where it needed to go *then*. Which is to beg the question, "Where does the church need to go *now*?"

It is five hundred years since the Reformation—five hundred years of a *sola Scriptura* church.

Does all of that work today as well as it did then?

The dominant statistics would clearly document that it isn't working.

When people are asked to report what is their chosen religion, today the most frequent response is "none." None! It isn't working!

Today, across the nation, 50 percent of the children in kindergarten are unchurched. Fifty percent! It isn't working!

Eighty percent of our congregations are stagnant or dying. It isn't working!

And the documentation could go on and on. It isn't working! It's time . . .

It's another five hundred years and it is time for a new evolution in the church.

Call it the twenty-first-century church or the emergent church or the postmodern church—whatever! It's time!

Here is my understanding of the twenty-first-century church from my study and observation:

The new authority of the church is now the Holy Spirit. The key question is not what is in the book, but where is the Holy Spirit leading the church? What is God trying to accomplish in this time and in this place?

So the authority shifts from a manual to the Holy Spirit—from a rule book to a dynamic presence that is moving and shaping and empowering and enlivening.

The new character of the church is driven by the Holy Spirit. It is alive and ever becoming. It is not fixed as in a rule book or a manual. It is flowing and free, liberating and compelling.

This new church is empowered by the Holy Spirit to be that fluid and dynamic entity able to be responsive and respectful.

Empowered now by the Holy Spirit that reaches into the soul of each and every individual, the church is now more individualized—not a "cookie cutter" church with one size fits all. Touching each and every life in its own sacred way, the Holy Spirit does not seek to homogenize, but to create a church that is free to be different and dynamic in a very personal level. Not at all corporate.

Worship now moves from a somewhat controlled and uniform activity to "an experience." Which is to say, when one comes to worship, what do they *experience*? The twenty-first-century worshipper is looking to experience the Holy—to experience unity with God—experience a fellowship that is real and genuine, united in God's Spirit—experience a sense of forgiveness, acceptance that is unconditional, empowered, and hopeful. Big time hopeful . . .

The nature of the church now becomes more open ended, evolving, ever new; not fixed or rigid in any way. Dynamic and flexible, capable of responding to the needs of its community and beyond.

The role of the clergy and church leaders is no longer to be the expert, the "one who knows"; but now to become a companion. "Don't tell me what to believe, how to understand the Scriptures . . . Help me find for myself what is God's plan for my life . . . Help me understand the Scriptures as they speak to me in my life and circumstance . . . Help me chart a course for my life that is pleasing to God . . . Help me find a moral code by which I can lead my life . . . Help me do it; don't tell me!"

Obedience shifts from a rule book or manual to the movement of the Holy Spirit in the life of the individual and the congregation. It is more open and empowering of the individual and therefore less rigid. It is also more compelling in the life of the congregation to be also open and flexible and responsive to the needs of others.

Therefore the opportunity for change is huge. One cannot keep the Holy Spirit in a box, or a rule book, or a manual. The Holy Spirit will not be contained. It is free to go as it desires, be all that it wants to be, and provoke and inspire all that it pleases.

Flexibility is one of the hallmarks of the twenty-first-century church. It is "contextual"—different in each setting and place. An urban congregation may look nothing like a rural or suburban congregation. The church is free to develop as the context in which it is found dictates and needs.

It is now the individual that is central in the twenty-first-century church. How is it going for each and every individual that this church encounters? One size does not fit all. How the church is and does will vary from person to person—which obviously creates a huge challenge to congregations. One way of worship will not fit all. One way of doing anything will not fit all. Either the congregation finds its niche and settles for that—or it provides a variety of worship and other opportunities to meet the needs of the varied population.

Being now centered in the Holy Spirit—now called *sola Spiritus*—the nature of the faith shifts. What is key now is not one's knowledge of the book, but rather one's *relationship* with God. How much do we really love Jesus? How close is our relationship with the Holy Spirit? How deeply do we allow God to penetrate into our hearts and souls—into our everyday lives? It's now all about relationships—with God—and with others.

It isn't how many Bible verses one knows. It isn't how much of the Bible one can recite. Instead it is the depth and quality of our relationship with the Holy that is the determining factor. Please understand, Scripture is a key tool to develop that relationship. The twenty-first-century church isn't against the Scriptures. They just don't hold the authority they used to hold.

Seriously, if you aren't Jewish, who has a kosher kitchen? Or do women keep quiet in church or keep their heads covered? We could go on and on. There are numerous verses in the Bible we no longer follow. Here's a classic example: Ephesians 6:5, "Slaves, be obedient to those who are your earthly masters, with fear and trembling, in singleness of heart, as to Christ . . ."

Clearly and without question, the Scriptures are essential to our growth in our relationship with God. We would not want to be without them. But they just do not represent the authority or command the obedience they once did.

God is our authority—which we gain through the Holy Spirit.

Religious formation is to develop an ever deeper and more passionate relationship with God—Father, Son and Holy Spirit. It is to let God be God more and more in our lives—in every bit of our lives—without reservation or hesitation.

So the church is now organized to provide those kinds of experiences and opportunities for deep spiritual development—open and flexible so that the Holy Spirit can move and impact us. Not rigid or fixed, repetitive or routine, constrained.

The new purpose of the church is salvation through surrender. Let God be God. Salvation is not our problem. Salvation is

God's gift fully realized here and now through the depth of that relationship with God.

More on the purpose of the church in the next chapter.

The focus of the twenty-first-century church is now on practice. "Don't tell me, *show me!*" Actions speak louder than words. Put the faith into movement and results. Make a difference. Demonstrate that relationship, don't just talk about it.

And this calls for a shift from "institutional" to "movement." The twenty-first-century church does not want to be bogged down with an institution—with policies and procedures, constitutions and bylaws, and all the rest.

The twenty-first-century church seeks to be liberated from all of that to become a movement.

Movement, I looked it up in the dictionary. A movement is people coming together for the sake of making a difference. Think of the civil rights movement, the environmental movement, the women's movement, the gay rights movement . . . People in action for a cause.

That's the kind of church the twenty-first-century church seeks to be. Alive and driven to make a visible difference.

"Look, all you church people want is my time and my money. I don't have enough time or enough money. Why should I get involved?"

Being a church in action, clearly and visibly making a difference in the life of a community is what the twenty-first-century church seeks.

And now orthodoxy becomes orthopraxis—from "right belief" to "right action." Show me! Make it real! Make a difference!

Attached is a graphic to picture what I am trying to describe in this chapter.

	Year 1,000 = Rome	Year 1500 = Reformation; Sola Scriptura	Year 2000 = Postmodern: Sola Spiritus
Authority for the Church	Rome	Scripture; manual, rule book	Holy Spirit
Character	Dictated	Rigid; black/white	Fluid/dynamic
Power	Rome	Book/congregation	Holy Spirit / individual
Worship	Spectator	Movement from spectator to participatory	To be experienced
Nature of the Church	Controlled	Determined	Open-ended; evolving; ever new
Role of the Pastor	Servant of Rome	Learned; Has answers	Companion; Helps me find my own answers
Obedience	Obedience to authority	Obedience to the Book	Obedience to the Holy Spirit; more open and empowering of the individual
Opportunity for Change	Not possible	Restricted	Open and dynamic
Flexibility	None	Limited	Yes; "contextual"—not all need to be alike
Empowering of the Individual	None	Limited	Empowering; encouraged to grow in the Spirit

Nature of the Faith	Dictated	Limited; didactic; book learning; How many Bible verses does one know?	Relational; relationship with God is more important than knowledge of the Book; not how many verses one knows but rather how deep is one's love of God!
Religion Formation	Dictated by Rome	Learn the Book! (confirmation)	Develop an ever-deepening relationship with God
Organization	Tightly controlled	Structured; defined (confined)	Flexible, open, contextual, dynamic
Purpose	Glorify God through Rome	Salvation through learning; knowing the Book	Salvation through relationship; being in love with God/Jesus
Focus	Doctrine	Scripture	Practice
Structure	Bound/controlled	Institutional; often focused on the survival of the institution	Movement; organized strictly for action; outreach
Orthodoxy (right belief)	Given by Rome	According to the Book	Not orthodoxy but orthopraxis

Copyright J. Fred Lehr

DISCUSSION

1. Brainstorm all the "radical shifts" the Reformation brought to the sixteenth-century church, like priests being able to marry, etc.

2. How shocking were these shifts to the folks back then—such dramatic changes from how the church operated for five hundred years?

3. What kind of resistance did these changes encounter?

4. How shocking will the changes brought by the postmodern church be for us today and what kind of resistance will result? How will we address that resistance?

Chapter Two

Main Thing, Gospel Centered, Kingdom Advancing

I HAVE SEVERAL AXIOMS that I live by. One of them is: You can't cure what you refuse to diagnose. We have done some serious diagnosing of the situation. Now it is time to address the "cure," the means to thrive in the twenty-first-century church.

First for me is a quote from Stephen Covey, the management guru: "The main thing is to keep the main thing the main thing."

From my training as an organizational development consultant, I know that where most organizations go wrong is by not being clear on their main purpose. Why does this organization exist?

So let's start there.

For me, the main thing can be said in two different ways—but it is still the one main thing.

One way to capture the main thing for the Christian church is to be excited about and faithful to the gospel of Jesus Christ.

And by "excited about and faithful to" I mean actions much more than words. In short, are we living the gospel and not just talking about it? Orthopraxis over orthodoxy!

And for me, in order to live the gospel means to live four things—and it's all four, not just one or two, but all four. This is not a smorgasbord. This is the gospel.

The first of the four things is the good news. The word gospel literally means good news—not bad news.

Therefore, the gospel cannot possibly be: "Unless you accept Jesus as your Lord and Savior you cannot go to heaven." That's not good news—that's bad news; and by very definition, cannot possibly be gospel.

Instead, the gospel is: "Jesus died and conquered death for you!" Now that's good news!

To make any requirement on our part to gain salvation is to condemn us. No matter what that requirement may be, I will never do it "enough."

Enough is a key word in my spiritual vocabulary. I am not on my own good enough to be fit for heaven. Only, exclusively by the merit of the life, death and resurrection of Jesus am I at all fit for heaven, period.

Therefore, I am set free from trying to "earn" my way, or "manipulate" my way into heaven. I am set free to embrace my salvation solely through Jesus, my Lord and Savior. I am free to celebrate my salvation. I am free and empowered to live my salvation in confidence and without fear. That's good news!

So the first of the four things that are gospel is the good news that empowers and liberates our lives.

The second thing is hope.

We normally seek our hope in all the wrong places—our finances, our education, our physical prowess, our good looks, our charm and personality, etc. And none of those are enduring—they are all temporary, they all can fail, none of them lasts forever.

But there is one source of hope that is dependable, durable, and cannot die. And that is Jesus Christ.

Jesus has conquered death—which is a key difference between resuscitation and resurrection. Lazarus was brought back to life again—he was resuscitated. But he still had death in his future.

Jesus is back to life again—but this time resurrected, with death now only in his past—death is no longer in his future.

There is no other contender for Lord and Savior who can make that claim. Jesus, and only Jesus, is the Risen Lord, resurrected, conqueror of death.

Therefore, when I place my hopes in Jesus, I have a source of hope that cannot die, that is stronger than death, that is forever. None can compare.

So to live hope is to share hope, enable hope, inspire hope for others—most especially those forgotten, disenfranchised, isolated, abused, and ignored. Those marginalized by society and are in desperate need of hope. We can give it to them through our Lord and Savior.

So the second thing in the gospel is hope.

The third thing is unconditional love.

Unconditional in two ways: without any conditions and beyond any conditions.

Without any conditions: Jesus never says, "I will love you if . . ." Jesus only says, "I will love you *regardless* . . ." Regardless! Nothing can stop Jesus' love for us. See Romans chapter 8!

God's love for us is unconditional—without any conditions.

But God's love for us is also beyond all conditions.

To say, "I love you" is to make a promise. Every promise on the face of this earth has at least three conditions:

1. Sincere

2. Capable

3. Death

Sincerity: am I sincere when I say "I love you" or am I being phony?

Am I capable of loving?

Will death stop my loving?

When I do a workshop on this topic, I like to illustrate it this way. At the end of the workshop I promise to give everyone there $100.

Now, am I sincere? You bet. I would love to pass out $100 bills. That would do wonders for my popularity.

Am I capable? Do I have a wallet full of hundred-dollar bills? *No*, but don't I wish!

But let's pretend that I do have all those hundred-dollar bills—will I still be alive at the end of this workshop? I could have a heart attack. A meteor could fall on my head. A crazy person could dash in and shoot me. None of those are likely, but they are all possible.

But when Jesus says, "I love you"—is he sincere? Or is he pulling our legs?

Anyone who will die for me is sincere. I can trust that person.

Is it possible for Jesus to love every man, woman and child alive today; every man, woman and child that ever was alive; and every man, woman and child that ever will be alive? Can anyone love that much?

Yes. Jesus is God—part of the Holy Trinity—Father, *Son*, and Holy Spirit. As God, Jesus can do whatever God wants to do—heal the sick, walk on water, calm the storm, change water into wine, whatever—even create a whole universe out of nothing! God can do whatever God wants to do.

And God has chosen—God has chosen to love every man, woman and child now alive, or was alive, or will be alive. God can do that because God is God. And no other entity can make that claim.

To live that unconditional love requires us to share unconditional love with all others—regardless! We dare not discriminate on any condition or circumstance. Jesus even taught us to love our enemies, do good to those who hate us. How's that for "regardless"?

And what about death? Can death stop Jesus from loving us?

No! And that is the key difference between resuscitation and resurrection.

Lazarus was resuscitated, alive again—but with death still in his future.

Jesus is alive again, but now with death only in his past. He is resurrected.

So death cannot stop Jesus from loving us. There is only one Risen Lord. No one else can make that claim.

Therefore, when Jesus promises to love us—he is sincere, capable, and death cannot stop him!

Unconditional love!

The fourth and last thing that is gospel from my point of view is an open future.

An open future means that my future does not depend on my past.

Regardless how sinful I have been, regardless how I have gone astray, regardless how minimal has been my faith—none of that has any power over the shape of my future in Jesus Christ.

God sets us free from our past to embrace the future that God wants us to have—a future ripe with promise, potential, possibilities, hope, freedom, love, and all that God intends for my life.

In God, all things are possible. All things are possible.

My future is not held captive to my past. I am free to be all that God wants me to be. And that's fabulous good news, that's gospel!

So one way to define the main thing, the purpose of the twenty-first-century church, is to vibrantly and actively live the gospel: good news, hope, unconditional love, and an open future.

The other way I like to define the main thing for the twenty-first-century church is to *grow and advance the* kingdom *of God.* This is a new reality that exemplifies good news, hope, unconditional love and an open future for all without exception.

One of the most frequent things mentioned by Jesus is the word "kingdom." Collectively, in Matthew, Mark, Luke and John, Jesus says the word "kingdom" about 120 times! One hundred twenty times! I guess Jesus really means it!

If that is a main thing for Jesus, then it also ought to be a main thing for the church.

To grow and advance the kingdom of God is an active thing—no spectator sport. We can't just talk about it and expect anything to happen. To faithfully and actively grow and advance the kingdom will require us doing something—like living the gospel!

Either way we put it—live the gospel: good news, hope, unconditional love and an open future *or* grow and advance the kingdom of God—we are saying the same thing.

The main thing is to keep the main thing the main thing.

That's where we start in our effort of move from a Reformation church (*sola Scriptura*) to a twenty-first-century church (*sola Spiritus*)!

DISCUSSION

1. Of the four (good news, hope, unconditional love, open future) which one(s) is our congregation strongest at doing (not just saying) and which are we weakest at? What tangible evidence is there?

2. What can we do to strengthen the ones we are weakest at? How can we make all four actionable?

3. How successful is our congregation at growing and advancing the kingdom of God? What evidence is there?

4. How can we improve our efforts to grow and advance the kingdom of God?

Chapter Three

Spiritual Maturity

IN THE LAST CHAPTER I presented the value of being centered in the gospel of Jesus Christ. That is where it all begins. And when we do that faithfully and with enthusiasm, the kingdom will grow and advance. Of that I am confident.

The next step is to deepen one's relationship with God through spiritual maturity.

Please note the graph:

Spiritual Maturity

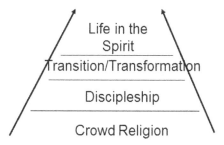

This captures in a graphic form what I want to present to help us better understand the process of spiritual maturity. My approach is based on the record in the New Testament regarding what happened to the first disciples—how they developed in their spiritual maturity and what that means for us.

Please note: this has nothing to do with the means of salvation. This is strictly helping us better understand spiritual maturity and what it looks like. How do we mature in our relationship with our Lord?

We begin in *crowd religion.*

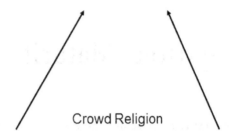

The New Testament records large crowds who gathered to hear Jesus. They came for a variety of reasons—to be inspired, entertained, healed, or just out of curiosity. Thousands came.

But out of the thousands, only a small number made any kind of commitment to become authentic disciples of Jesus.

Even so in our congregations today. We can pack the pews, but how many of those in attendance actually make the decision to be a genuine follower of our Lord along with all that such a commitment entails? The answer is—way too few. And that's a key to our problem.

To grow and advance the kingdom is to invite and encourage people to step out of the crowd and become disciples.

The crowd is what is normal in a society. The crowd is simply being just like everyone else. If in our self-analysis we see ourselves the same as all those around us, odds are that we are still a part of the crowd and have not made any sincere commitment to be a faithful disciple of Jesus.

Being a disciple means living by a new standard and set of values. It means taking the leap to dare to attempt to diligently live by the teachings of Jesus, the example of Jesus, and the ways of the kingdom.

It is a serious decision that is life changing. So if our lives have not been changed, if we look like everyone else—then most likely we remain in the crowd and have not taken the critical step to move from the crowd into *discipleship*.

If our prayer life is minimal, if we have no serious impressions of many of the teachings of the church, if we are marginal in our commitments to the church, if we allow many of the pressures of daily life to take a higher place than our faith in our lives—then we are very likely members of the crowd.

In the twenty-first-century church, we will make that continual invitation to step out of the crowd and discover the joy and empowerment that becoming a disciple entails. We will model and encourage those in our pews to become more than "just like everyone else," but to become the kind of disciple that Jesus called.

So the first step in spiritual maturity is to move out of the crowd and accept the joys and responsibilities of being a disciple—an active agent to grow and advance the kingdom.

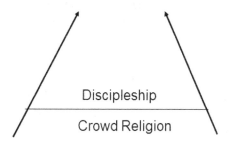

Discipleship

Crowd Religion

That movement is no small thing. There is safety in the crowd. It is more comfortable to be just like everyone else. We won't stand out. We won't be different. We will more easily fit in with others. We risk sacrificing our popularity if we dare to become a disciple. We may even risk other opportunities and engagements by daring to be different.

When someone musters the courage to move into discipleship, we need to honor that and congratulate them and embrace them into the work of the kingdom.

Please note: the most important duty of a disciple is to make other disciples. So a quick litmus test to discover whether one is a disciple or not is to ask if that person is actively about the work of making new disciples, of growing and advancing the kingdom.

Now there are many, many ways to make new disciples. Remember, guilting or threatening someone with eternal hell is not consistent with the gospel. Those strategies are the opposite of the gospel—they are "bad news," not good news.

So they are not in our methodology of growing and advancing the kingdom. The best strategy is to model the life of a disciple, to put the teachings of Jesus into the way we authentically live our lives. To just "be" a disciple is the best way to make new disciples by inviting and encouraging others. "They will know we are Christians by our love . . . "

Now we need to immediately say that discipleship is not where it ends. In fact, it is just where it begins.

Discipleship is actually an elementary form of spiritual maturity. I sometimes call it the "Sunday School Theology" that fits children but will not satisfy a mature hunger for the kingdom.

Discipleship is where we begin our journey toward spiritual maturity.

While thousands gathered in the crowds to hear Jesus—how many does the New Testament record actually became disciples? The number is seventy or seventy-two. Jesus sent out the seventy to the towns and villages to tell others about the kingdom.

So if Jesus could only get seventy disciples out of the crowds of thousands, what can we expect to do? However, Jesus did not work with the same congregation week after week. Jesus was itinerant and moved from place to place, never staying in one place very long, as we are called to stay and witness over the years.

We can't hide behind those numbers. Disciples make disciples, period.

Rejoice with a new disciple, but understand that the process of spiritual maturity has only just begun.

As the days passed, eventually the disciples began to argue with each other over who was the best or who would get the best seats in the kingdom. This is a testimony to the shallowness of their maturity.

Yes, they stepped out from the crowd—which needs to be celebrated. Well done! But that is just the beginning.

This is my main concern with much of the conversation about making disciples. Too often we say that being a disciple is the end goal. "You are a disciple. You made it. Congratulations." That's my problem.

Please keep in focus that discipleship is the beginning, not the end. There is a deeper maturity awaiting.

As the years with Jesus unfolded, eventually the journey led to the garden of Gethsemane. There, when Jesus needed his friends the most, every single disciple either betrayed, denied, or abandoned Jesus.

When our faith is seriously put to the test, we are often found weak and insufficient in our commitment to our Lord.

Too easily we fall back into the ways of the crowd, the ways of the familiar and the "safe," the ways of the comfortable and secure.

Too easily we fail to advance the kingdom. We are masters at making excuses not to recruit new disciples, not to do the work of the kingdom, not to make the personal sacrifice.

Too easily we accept that being a disciple is enough and that our spiritual journey is at a "good enough" place.

Too easily we sacrifice the best and accept the merely good enough.

In the garden we discover that our discipleship was not all that we thought it was. We become painfully aware of that short-coming. We confess our faults and failures and seek renewal and forgiveness.

Note: it is only safe to become so radically honest with our-selves when we are equally confident in God's unconditional love and endless forgiveness and mercy. It is only safe to be penitent when we know full well that Jesus has already died for our sins and the grace we so dearly desire is ours without condition.

Transition or *transformation* is that stage of spiritual maturity when we testify to our failure to be all that God wants us to be.

We have done what we shouldn't have done—and we have failed to do what God wanted us to do. We have sinned by commission and omission. And we seek forgiveness and a deeper relationship with our Lord.

While this is not a comfortable place in our spiritual maturity, it is a good place and a place we can be in peace. The discomfort is a testimony of our growing maturity. It is a blessing to become honest with ourselves and be set free from the delusion of having attained all that we can attain in the spiritual journey.

Knowing full well that I am far from perfect is liberating. I am no longer pretending. I have dared to embrace the truth of my imperfection—and that sets me free to be real. I have the confidence in God's unconditional love that sustains me in my confessions and lifts my hearts with God's relentless pursuit of my soul. It is not a comfortable place to be—but it is a good place to be. And God sustains me and supports me and lifts me in the discomfort.

Yes, I am a sinner. But I can claim that in confidence and in unreserved hope and love.

Finally, we see the final stage of spiritual maturity as recorded in the New Testament.

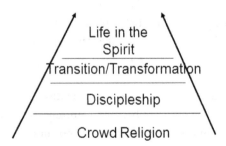

Notice, the graph narrows. From the seventy who became disciples, now only twelve are recorded as having reached what I call *life in the Spirit*.

This time in the journey of the disciples is Pentecost.

After Pentecost, all twelve will lay their lives on the line for the sake of the kingdom. Everyone of them dies rather than deny their Lord.

Remember, this is not the path to salvation. Salvation is entirely different. This is merely and only the path to spiritual maturity.

Life in the Spirit is the complete and entire surrender of one's life to the work of the kingdom. Obviously in God's economy, all of us don't need to reach this level. It is reserved for a few—the Mother Teresas or the Rev. Dr. Martin Luther Kings of our time.

While it is a level of maturity I hope to obtain, I know that I am primarily at transition/transformation. And that is okay.

Growth in the Spirit is not something we control. It is a gift of the Spirit. God grants us this maturity. We do not achieve it on our own.

So we seek to more and more surrender to God's will, to pursue a deeper and deeper relationship with our Lord, to reach for a greater and greater immersion in the Spirit—but only God can grant it.

Continue to seek. Pray. Study. Surrender. And then let God be God and appreciate that it is better that God is in control and not us!

The primary purpose for me including this in this book is to put forward the idea that one of the main reasons we are not as successful as we could be in becoming a twenty-first-century church is our failure to recruit more disciples.

We try to attract the crowd, but do we provide the opportunity and environment to make it possible for folks to step our from the crowd and into discipleship? Do we faithfully model discipleship ourselves?

And if we have disciples, do we create a safe place that gives them the opportunity to be honest with themselves so that all can dare to embrace our shortcomings and confess our faults and failures openly and freely? Do we support each other in our transition/transformation? Or do we pretend that discipleship is the final goal and stay stuck at that level?

When we gather as the family of faith, what kind of experiences do we provide that would enable the movement from the crowd to discipleship or from discipleship to transition/

transformation or even the ultimate complete and total surrender to life in the Spirit?

What is it like when we gather? Are we too comfortable being like everyone else and resist taking the risks of discipleship, transition/transformation, or life in the Spirit?

Faith is that leap out of our comfort zones into a new life in Jesus. How are we supporting and enabling each other to take that leap?

Note below the Spiritual Life Survey. It is a tool I developed to help each of us determine where we are in our own spiritual journey.

SPIRITUAL LIFE SURVEY

In completing the statements below, choose that response that *best* expresses how you *really function* (how you behave), *not* how you think you *ought* to function or what you should do or what would be ideal. *Be completely honest!* Select the response that *best* describes you.

1. My approach to *life* is:
    a. Life gives you what it gives you; it's all a matter of circumstances. God plays no active part anymore. Live accordingly.
    b. If I obey and perform well, I will be rewarded; if I disobey, I will be punished. Keep in mind that "Ledger Book" in heaven.
    c. Life is a struggle filled with many challenges; it is a quest for a goal; a sense of being incomplete, a movement to fulfill the quest. Be better every day.
    d. Life is a gift from God; a privilege to be enjoyed, used for others and celebrated. God made us for God's purpose. My life is lived accordingly.

2. My view of *afterlife* is:
    a. I'm not sure there is an afterlife—it doesn't really affect the way I live.

    b.   A final judgment based on performance with reward or punishment; heaven or hell. I fear hell, so I live to get into heaven.

    c.   A final appeal to God's mercy; salvation by grace and not merit. I live trusting in the Lord, for I know I am a sinner.

    d.   Something to be reckoned with seriously but not fearfully; a transition to being complete. I live in quiet joy and confidence.

3. When I *pray*, I see it as:

    a.   I really do not pray regularly.

    b.   An opportunity to place my concerns before God.

    c.   Response "b" plus a striving for a closer relationship with Christ. Confession.

    d.   Responses "b" and "c" plus celebrating the fullness of life; glorifying God. Giving praise and thanksgiving

4. My *view of the world* is:

    a.   I have no certain view of the world; *or*, my view is secular and not spiritual at all.

    b.   Fairly optimistic; generally the good wins over the evil so that I live depending on my good deeds to really make a difference.

    c.   Evil rules this earth and the good awaits final vindication (final recognition and reward) in God's coming kingdom. The world is to be patiently endured.

    d.   The world is a temporal stage of tragedy and comedy, bad and good. It is a place to seek justice, to witness to the gospel, to celebrate in quiet joy and confidence. So I live out that pursuit of justice for others. I am an active witness for God and I live in contentment and peace.

5. To me, *love* is:

    a.   I'm not sure; *or*, I don't care; *or*, I don't really think about it.

    b.   Tenderness and warmth—a kind of romantic love shared between people.

     c.   Self sacrifice; Christ on the cross. I live to give myself to others. Delayed gratification to benefit others.

     d.   Building each other up; living to love again in a new way, more than self sacrifice. A very deep sense of personal commitment, even unto death. Seeking community and genuine fellowship.

6. To me, *sin* is:

     a.   I have no real idea; never thought much about it.

     b.   Occasionally puzzling; means that I missed the mark somehow. I really am a good person who obeys God and does not do wrong very often.

     c.   A power that is within me that wars against my good intentions. I know I am a sinner, though I struggle to be less sinful.

     d.   Already defeated by Christ for me; yet I still have to wrestle with it, only now with a strong sense of confidence. I sin, for which I am sorry, but I do not feel victimized by my sinfulness, thanks to God.

7. The *Holy Spirit* has *given me*:

     a.   I really don't know; I'm not sure I care.

     b.   A healthy nature ready to grow and develop. I am a believer who proudly obeys God.

     c.   A new presence of God in my life; nurturing, supporting, confronting. I am not satisfied with my spiritual waywardness and the Spirit affirms and loves me as I struggle with my shortcomings.

     d.   A new community of faith (the church); new life, freedom, purpose, strength. God active in my life, molding my life and guiding my decisions and actions. I have a deep and profound confidence in the guidance of the Spirit.

8. In my *faith life*, I would say I am:

     a.   Faith is not my strong point. I am not sure what I believe or how my faith changes or shapes my life.

b. Confident that I believe, yet knowing that there are moments of doubt. As a believer, the doubting confuses me; but by obeying God, I am put right again.

c. Critical of myself. I need to lean on God. My faith life is an ongoing quest to be more like Christ.

d. Mature, accepting, free; I am sure that all things really do work together for the good for all those who love God.

9. In my *relationships* with *other people*, I:

a. Am like most people, not very different. It pays to be very careful in one's relationships. Don't get hurt.

b. Follow the Golden Rule. I am a good person who treats people nicely and politely and people are usually nice to me.

c. Am willing to practice self denial; delayed gratification for the other's sake. In my quest to be a better person, being for others as Christ was for us is my goal.

d. Accept suffering as a part of all human relationships; yet I still prefer working with others rather than going it alone.

10. As I see it, *my agenda* in life is:

a. To earn money, seek security, have a nice family.

b. To do good and avoid evil (reward and punishment so that I may go to heaven and not to hell). Obey God.

c. To struggle to be authentic and true. To overcome my sinfulness.

d. To be obedient to God's plan over any and every human plan; serving all people, because I love.

11. To me, *knowledge/understanding/truth* is:

a. Whatever the world determines it to be.

b. Information, data, facts, empirical; from the five senses; numbers, science.

c. A growing sense of something beyond in tension with the empirical/factual/date. No longer satisfied with my own sense of knowing. Truth is to be pursued; a quest.

     d.   Spiritual enlightenment rather than the empirical/ factual; God's agenda over any/all human agendas. Worldly knowledge is not at all satisfactory.

12. As I experience it, the *Christian community* is:

     a.   Confusing to me; I have never really experienced it.

     b.   A hearty fellowship with those who try to do good.

     c.   A mutual journey, sharing a common spirit, in quest of the truth.

     d.   Believers bound solidly together in Christ's love and a mutual commitment to enhance each other for the sake of doing God's work.

13. I see *myself* as:

     a.   I'm not sure of myself image; *or*, I see it in secular terms based on my vocation or financial status.

     b.   A child of God; I am trying to do good and avoid evil.

     c.   Both saint and sinner; hopeless yet hopeful; adopted, saved by God's grace.

     d.   An heir to God's kingdom; an energized agent of redemption; one who seeks to be a healer in an ailing world.

14. Regarding my *self worth*, I am:

     a.   Measured by my worldly success, financial status, political power, popularity.

     b.   Confident that I do more good than bad.

     c.   Gaining confidence in God's acceptance and counting on God's forgiveness.

     d.   Accepted and acceptable; granted purely by God's grace.

15. As I experience it, the *Lord's Supper (Holy Communion)* is:

     a.   I never really think about it; *or*, I am not sure; *or*, I really don't care.

     b.   A way to remember the past (Christ's death and resurrection) and a hope for victory in the future (heaven).

     c.   The real presence of Christ's body and blood given to forgive my sins.

    d.   Christ's real presence creating a new community of faith and love in mission. It pulls us together in the mystery and majesty of the sacrament and moves us to service for others.

All the "a" responses are Crowd Religion.

All the "b" responses are Discipleship.

All the "c" responses are Transition/Transformation.

All the "d" responses are Life in the Spirit.

You may be at different places in different aspects of your spiritual life. That is okay.

Where are you now? Where would you like to be?

Pray and ask for God's guidance.

DISCUSSION

1. How can we utilize the Spiritual Life Survey in our congregation so that many members will have some sense of where they are in their own spiritual maturity? Who will be responsible for managing this process?

2. What can we do better to assist folks in crowd religion to move to discipleship? How will we put that into action?

3. How can we better create a safe environment for disciples to come to terms with the transition/transformation "confession" that enables that spiritual growth? Who will lead that effort?

4. How can we make spiritual maturity a foundational and essential part of our congregation's ministry? Who will make that happen?

Chapter Four

From *Sola Scriptura* to *Sola Spiritus*

LET ME BE PERFECTLY clear—*no one* wants to get rid of the Bible. The Holy Scriptures are precious to us and an essential resource for faith development, a precious window into the will of God. We need to know how we got here—how has the faith developed over the centuries—and what was important when and why. *Do not* abandon the Scriptures.

At the same time, we need to come to terms with the reality that the Scriptures no longer carry the authority they once did. An evolutionary process is unfolding that seeks more guidance by the Holy Spirit than guidance from a "rule book or manual."

A classic example of this is the openness to same-sex relationships. Clearly, that cannot be supported by Scripture alone. In fact, there are some strong arguments found in Scripture that oppose it.

But the church, and especially the twenty-first-century church, has determined that God is calling us to be welcoming to same-sex relationships and no longer condemns them.

It reminds me of my youth in the '50s and '60s when folks were using Scripture to argue against the civil rights of African Americans and other minorities or the liberation of women's rights. At that time, there were strong opinions, documented by Scripture, to support keeping the status quo.

But, thanks be to God, those arguments did not prevail. The status quo was seen as unjust. And freedom was embraced over prejudice and oppression.

In the exact same way today is the twenty-first-century church against being held captive by a rule book or manual when the Spirit of God is moving among us and guiding us in new directions.

The twenty-first-century church is calling us to a more open, inclusive, dynamic, and fluid means of being the church.

Instead of a one-size-fits-all approach that lays down dos and don'ts that no longer make sense to God's people, the twenty-first-century church seeks the fresh air of a more flexible and creative way to serve God and be God's people.

Another aspect of this is the emphasis on the individual in an interesting way. The twenty-first-century church is far more focused on the individual.

People do not want to be told the dos and don'ts. Instead they seek a way to determine the particular dos and don'ts that fit their life at this time and in this place.

Yes, this is a real relativism—what is relative for me that may not be relative for you? What makes sense for my life that may not fit for anyone else's life?

And more specifically, what is God calling me to do with my life that may not work at all for your life? And how do I determine that? Will a rule book or manual tell me that? Or will a deep and personal relationship with my Lord be a far more effective way for me to chart the course of my life, to find a moral code to direct my days and deeds, to seek a personal definition about who I am to be and how I am to prioritize my life?

It is that personal, deep, and passionate relationship with the Holy that makes a great deal more sense to the twenty-first-century church that some rigid and inflexible rule book written long, long ago.

Can an ancient text be relevant when the knowledge of humanity and the world is so radically different than when that ancient text was written? Saint Paul was a tremendous person. But he could not possibly know what we know today. For one, he fully believed that Christ would return soon, possibly within his lifetime, and that had a huge impact on his faith. We know that the immanent return did not happen. Saint Paul got it wrong. In what other ways did the authors of that ancient text get it wrong? How can we rely only on such a resource?

Instead, the twenty-first-century church wants a resource that is current, alive, active in their personal lives, dynamic, and compelling in direct ways. They want it real and they want it now.

A rigid and fixed rule book or manual will not suffice. It is important, please understand. It is extremely helpful to know where we come from to help us understand where we need to go. But it does not carry the authority for "my life now" that it once had. We just need to understand that.

So instead of insisting that "the Scriptures say" as the guiding principle, we need a different method.

Let me explain this with a real-life story.

In the mid-1980s I went on an Outward Bound expedition. That's the kind of event where a bunch of strangers come together, go into the wilderness, and hope they all come back alive.

Among the twelve participants in my group, I was the only clergy. I didn't go there to be a religious authority. In fact, my goal was to be set free from that burden and have an opportunity to just be myself. However, that was taken from me in the first ten minutes of the event.

As we introduced ourselves to each other, we asked the three natural questions: Who are you? Where do you come from? What do you do?

What do you do? "I'm a parish pastor."

"Oh, good, now we know we'll all be safe." No joke. Someone actually said that. "Now we know we'll all be safe." We have a "holy person" in our midst. Truly God would not let calamity befall a holy person. We will be safe.

Among the twelve there were three or four who had been hurt by the church and were anti anything to do with the church. They began to attack me with various accusations.

At first I got defensive and tried to argue back. But I quickly realized that arguing back wasn't working and it wasn't fun. So I shifted to saying instead, "I hear you, but this is how it is for me."

"This is what my faith does for me. This is what I get out of being a part of a faith community. This is what believing in Jesus does for me." And so forth . . .

Time and time again these wounded souls kept bringing up issues of faith and the church. I never initiated that conversation. I wasn't there for that. But each time I responded, "I hear you, but this is how it is for me."

But what blew me away was on our last evening together, as we were giving feedback to each other about how it was to be on this expedition with each other—every one of the antagonists said, "Now that I have gotten to know you, I am thinking about going back to church."

Now that someone did not quote a rule book or a manual . . .

Now that someone did not guilt them or judge them . . .

Now that someone spoke to them from his/her life, from his/her heart instead of from a place of authority or orthodoxy . . .

Now that they were respected and met as equals . . .

Now that they were given the honor of being heard . . .

Now that the conversation was on a relational level and not quoting from a rule book . . .

They were open to hear . . .

They were open to reconsider . . .

They were open to be changed . . .

They were open to be touched at a deeper place in their lives, in their souls . . .

I am convinced that it wasn't my fantastic personality or anything particularly outstanding about me—I'm just an ordinary guy.

I am convinced that it was the genuine respect and high regard in which I held their positions while at the same time being open and caring enough to share from the depth within my soul.

"This is how it is for me . . ." That was the magic, more than my stellar personality.

And that's the key to the twenty-first-century church.

Don't tell me . . . Don't guilt me . . . Don't hit me with a bunch of quotes from a rule book or a manual.

Just reach out to me from your heart, from your soul . . .

Be real . . . Be caring . . . Be honest . . . And *listen*!

That's what the twenty-first-century church hungers for. And we are not very good at delivering it.

In most of the congregations I know, that level of conversation rarely happens. I even proposed that we introduce that kind of discourse in our common greetings of each other.

When we gather on a Sunday morning, or whenever, instead of just saying, "How are you?" Let's also say, "How is it going for you? What has been your faith struggle this week? How are you and God getting along with each other?"

When I proposed that, the congregation was terrified. That kind of interaction was seen as radical and unheard of. And I suppose they were right.

In some critical ways, it is radical. But so is the resurrection from the dead!

Stuck in a rule book or manual and failing to be open and honest about our faith—strengths and weaknesses—failing to be together on a deeper, relational level—is what the twenty-first-century church now holds against us.

Superficial won't cut it any more. It needs to be personal. It needs to be relational.

It needs to be inviting—encourage each other into an ever deeper and deeper relationship with our Lord. And it is in that relationship that we find the Truth to guide our lives.

It is in the depth of that sacred relationship that we can discover what God expects from us—who we are to be for ourselves and for each other.

It is in the depth of that holy dialogue with God that we will define that moral code for our lives.

That's what the twenty-first-century church desires. And in the vast majority of our congregations, it does not exist.

We need to find ways to make that kind of conversation as comfortable and as normal as asking how we are or all the customary stuff.

We need to structure our time together to enable deeper relational interactions.

We need to facilitate a way to be open to each other—and open to those outside the church. This is what evangelism needs to capture.

"This is what it's like for me . . . How is it for you? How can we grow in our faith in a deep and personal way? How can we support each other in this spiritual quest? What does the church need to do to enable this holy endeavor?"

Whether we like it or not, we live in a "me" culture. The basic questions of this current culture are something like: "Why should I? What's in it for me? What will I get out of it? What is it going to cost me?"

While I am very uncomfortable with such an approach, I know that it's real. And we aren't going to change that any time soon.

So let's understand that emphasis and respond properly.

"Why should you? Well, this is what it's like for me. This is what I get out of it. This is what it means for my life. This is what I would miss if Jesus was not in my life. This is what I would miss if I did not belong to a faith community."

That's a huge change we need to make to move from *sola Scriptura* to *sola Spiritus*. It's an enormous change. It is a cultural change with the existing church.

The resistance will be every bit as severe as it was when Luther launched the Reformation. We can expect that.

But 80 percent of our congregations are stagnant or dying.

Fifty percent of the children in kindergarten are unchurched.

What we are doing is not working.

Dr. Phil on television asks a good question: "How's that working for you?"

Church, *sola Scriptura* is not working for us any more. It was perfectly right five hundred years ago. Luther and the other Reformers got it right. No question.

But it's five hundred years later. And it is time for another evolution of God's dynamic and alive church.

DISCUSSION

1. In what ways have we allowed the Scriptures to be used as a "rule book and manual"? What are the benefits of that? What are the negative aspects of that?

2. How can we embrace the Scriptures in a way that is not "controlling" or "constraining" but more liberating and inspiring?

3. In what ways can our congregation embrace the notion that the Scriptures are more of a valuable guide than a rigid rule book—an essential resource for life, but not a means of judgment and condemnation?

4. When we do Bible Study at our congregation, are we open to individuals coming to various insights; seeking God's guidance for their own lives—or do we insist on one right interpretation?

Chapter Five

Making an Experience

THE TWENTY-FIRST-CENTURY CHURCH SEEKS an experience.

Having Sunday worship, or any other part of our religious life, being routine or repetitive just does not work for the twenty-first-century church.

They are not looking for a tired tradition. They want a dynamic and alive experience.

This is another great shift. I have been ordained for over forty years and have never been taught to look at worship as an experience. But that is exactly what the twenty-first-century church expects.

When today's worshippers arrive, they are looking for a new experience. They don't just want to hear about the good news, hope, unconditional love and an open future. They want to experience it.

What kind of experience are we providing whenever we worship?

Let's take it step by step.

I am a retired pastor, so I get to belong to a congregation without the responsibilities of the role of pastor. My experience at the congregation I belong is not always the best. Just walking from my car into the church building, many of our members do not even make eye contact, let alone say hello or any other greeting. So the very first experience is not even welcoming, let alone unconditional love. Inside, we have designated greeters so that at least someone says hello.

As a traditionalist myself, I prefer the familiar liturgical form we follow most every Sunday; but I do notice that it lacks quite a bit of enthusiasm. It is well done, but one would not call it dynamic or exciting. It is hardly a vibrant experience of good news.

My pastor's sermons are usually well done and thoughtful, but not always challenging. And I know from experience that many parishioners would rather have a comforting sermon than a challenging one. So I appreciate the pastor's desire to respond to the needs of the members.

The music at our congregation is well done—one of the best parts of our ministry. But the experience is more passive than active. We sing hymns, but not with a lot of gusto.

I suspect what I experience is quite typical of many congregations. Worship is done well in a traditional or even contemporary sense. But when it comes to being a "dynamic experience" (emotional and experiential vs. scripted and formal), something is missing.

What if we structure all our gatherings at the congregation with an eye to the kind of *experience* we are providing?

From the moment anyone arrived on the property, do they *experience* the notion that they are truly welcomed there and are greeted warmly by everyone?

As they enter the door, do they have to find where to go and what to do on their own, or are they met with someone who will do more than just say hello?

As they approach the worship space, are they given enough of a guide so that they can follow the worship even if they have never been there before? In our congregation, we jump all around the hymnal and bounce around the bulletin in a way that only the initiated would understand. A complete newcomer would be befuddled by it all. Not a positive experience.

Does the worship itself communicate on a level even the most novice of attenders would understand, or is it only for the initiated and ones already accustomed to our style? Another negative experience.

We have Holy Communion at each service which, as one who is on the "in crowd," I greatly appreciate. But if someone who is not "trained in our system" would dare to take the brave step of showing up at our worship, would Holy Communion communicate anything they would understand, or would that also be a bit off putting? Bad experience unless it is carefully presented.

We could go on and on. Way too much of what we do when we gather as Christians is designed for the initiated and long-time members. Far too little is designed for the total novice who may have mustered the courage to dare to enter our doors. What kind of experience is that?

And even for the initiated—I want to reflect on the experience of Holy Communion. In my faith, Jesus is *really present* as he promises in the bread and in the cup ("This is my body . . ."). The traditional response upon receiving the elements of bread and wine are to say, "Amen" ("Yes, Lord, let it be so.") That's a fine thing to say—but rather tired these days and often just repeated without much emotion.

What if instead, when we receive the body of Christ, we said, "Wow!" Truly, if anything in life is a genuine "wow moment," having the true body of Christ placed right in my hand qualifies. And how would that change the dynamics of the experience?

Instead of a routine "amen," we joyfully exclaimed a heartfelt "wow!" Trust me; I've had congregations do that and it makes things far more joyous and uplifting—has brought people to smile—and even tears. That's an experience!

We need to rethink every aspect of our lives as congregations. What kind of experiences are we providing to those who come into our presence? Do we genuinely and clearly provide opportunities to experience good news, hope, unconditional love and an open future?

Open future? When 80 percent of our congregations are stagnant or dying, there's not much open future existing there!

Every moment, every interaction, every aspect of our life as a congregation needs to undeniably reflect that good news, hope, unconditional love and open future that the gospel of Jesus uniquely provides. I have a strong belief that making this adjustment alone will profoundly improve the life of a congregation and make it a far more attractive place to belong.

And not just within the confines of the congregation campus, but extending out into the community; do those who live in the surrounding community identify our faith fellowships as empowered centers of good news, hope, unconditional love and an open future? Want to know? *Ask them.*

And when we ask them what they think or know about our ministries, I suspect we will be very disappointed in their answers. Answers like: "I have no idea? Oh, is that a church? I know nothing about them."

Generally, we are pathetically poor at extending even the good that happens within our fellowships out into the surrounding communities. Only those within "the club" know what it is all about. What kind of experience is that?

I served a congregation in northern Vermont for most of the 1980s. When I arrived they had just gone through a difficult time and they were so financially distressed they considered closing. We worked together for nine years. During those nine years we doubled the size of the building, launched a nonprofit agency and started a daughter congregation. Notice I said *we* did that, not me.

One of the keys to that success was an important attitude. At my first meeting with the governing board of the congregation I was firmly informed that they had only one policy: Don't get into a rut.

Don't get into a rut. Keep it alive and dynamic. Keep it from getting routine and stale. Make it welcoming and affirming as well as challenging and on the cutting edge.

It was a place where folks made a sincere effort to really get to know each other. Coffee hour was just that—a full sixty minutes of just chatting with each other and showing God's love for each other. Is there any wonder why the congregation did so well? The experience they provided was warm and authentic, fully demonstrating good news, hope, unconditional love and an open future. Try it. You'll like it!

DISCUSSION

1. When we come to worship at our congregation, what kind of experiences do we have? Do we *always* experience good news, hope, unconditional love and an open future?

2. In all honesty, how is the love expressed in our congregation not *unconditional* (without any conditions) but rather *conditional* (fitting into our conditions—doing things our way)? How can we change that?

3. If someone who has never been to any church service before in their entire lives comes to our congregation for worship, what kind of experience will that be for them? Will they know what to do and when? How awkward will that be for them—how uncomfortable? How can we address that?

4. How much of our worship is designed for the initiated "members of the club" and how much for folks who have never been to any church before? Is that okay?

Chapter Six

Clergy,
from Expert to Companion

IN THE TWENTY-FIRST-CENTURY CHURCH the role of the clergy will shift from being an "expert" to being a "companion."

We believe that *sola Scriptura* began to unravel sometime in the 1960s. That was a time when all authority came into question. Especially with the Vietnam War and the whole Watergate scandal, confidence in authority was eroded and diminished.

Even so with the clergy. Around that time we also began to read in the press and hear on the television about the scandal of clergy with adultery, child abuse and financial schemes. The church was rocked and images tumbled.

This fed even more into the cultural shift that the twenty-first-century church was unfolding and gave it extra momentum. It was not the sole cause, but a strong, contributing factor.

Therefore, the role of the clergy now takes a profound shift.

Under *sola Scriptura*, the clergy were to be the resident experts on the Scriptures and all things holy. They were well trained—in most mainline denominations requiring a master's degree. In small towns, the pastor was one of the better educated members of the community. There was considerable respect held in that holy office.

But things shifted. And now the Holy Office of Word and Sacrament no longer holds the same level of confidence and trust. Now folks no longer accept that the pastor is the expert—especially on all matters concerning *their* spiritual lives.

In the twenty-first-century church, people do not want to be told—or will accept being told—what the Holy expects from them or what it means to be a believer. In the twenty-first-century church, individuals want to discover that for themselves.

Therefore, the role of the clergy is not to *tell*, but rather to *assist*. Not to *educate* or *inform*, but rather to *guide* and *accompany*.

It is far better for the clergy in the twenty-first-century church to take the role of fellow traveler on this spiritual journey than as an expert authority. Seeking the *sola Spiritus* can be a venture of equal partners.

It is far better to exercise a role of just another seeker who may have some additional training in the quest, than as a full master of the subject.

This will shape some aspects of the clergy role. For example preaching: rather than pontificating from the pulpit like some knowledgeable academic, it would be better to say, "This is how it is for me . . ."—a lesson I learned in Outward Bound.

Rather than approaching teaching Scripture or other aspects of the faith from the perspective of "here are *the* answers . . . ," instead one might point out that the church at various times in its development held various assumptions over the centuries, and today we are learning new perspectives which one can grasp for themselves. Again, "Here's how it is for me . . . ," rather than, "Let me tell you . . ."

In evangelism and other outreach, presenting oneself as a fellow seeker who has found something that works for them is desired far more than the "believe this or go to hell" approach.

D. T. Niles has a great definition of evangelism: "One beggar telling another beggar where to find the food." Excellent.

From a posture of humility and modesty, the clergy need to present ourselves as ones who hunger every bit as much as anyone else for the Sacred in their lives.

For in the twenty-first-century church it isn't knowledge of the Holy that is valued. It is the depth and breadth and quality of the *relationship* with the Holy that is respected. And we do not communicate that *relationship* through academics or didactic brilliance. We do it by the means of living our lives.

Clergy are now more than ever measured by what they are doing with their lives. "Don't tell me; show me . . ." is the mantra of the twenty-first-century church.

Clergy will more and more be required to lead by example, not by scholarship.

And a heartfelt exploration of the faith will carry more weight that a brilliant exposition of even the most complex theological formulas.

Make it real. Make it something folks can feel and experience. That is the challenge of the clergy—and the church in the twenty-first century.

In preaching, I would take the approach of exploring what is it in the text that touches the lives of the congregation from one's own personal lens; how it can impact their spiritual health; the options of the ways of the world or the ways of the Spirit; and help the congregation apply the filter of good news, hope, unconditional love and an open future to this task.

Ideas alone are not sufficient. Action does speak quite louder than words—especially now.

Preaching and teaching are more an exercise of sharing from one's soul than of erudite eloquence.

Make it real—and from the center of our beings. Make it a living demonstration of the full gospel—good news, hope, unconditional love and an open future—in our lives.

Back it up with action. Make it evident. Make it a living testimony.

And not just the clergy, but the ministry as a whole will be judged by its effectiveness to model and present that living gospel far more than its ability to articulate a knowledgeable argument.

Lead by example—that's the demand of the twenty-first-century church.

Make it real. "Show me . . ."

"Journey with me, Pastor. Share with me your insights and struggles as I share with you mine. Together, let's seek the truth. Side-by-side, let's enrich our relationship with the Holy and let it sink deeply into our souls. As companions, let's learn to live the faith more authentically."

If anything, just point me in the right direction, stay by my side so I don't go off in a hurtful direction, but let me make the discoveries for myself. Be my guide and companion, not my tutor or expert.

DISCUSSION

1. How much do we expect our clergy to be "experts" rather than fellow members on a spiritual journey? Is that helpful or distracting?

2. How can we support our clergy in the effort to shift from an expert to a companion? What would that look like? What resistance would we encounter?

3. How can we develop an environment at our congregation that enables all of us to see ourselves as pilgrims on a spiritual journey—seeking every day to more fully embrace God's call to be all that God wants us to be?

4. How can we enable our members to see themselves as companions to those who do not now have a deep and personal relationship with Jesus?

Chapter Seven

From Uniform to Contextual

WHEN I GREW UP in my denomination, one could go from church to church and find worship pretty much all the same. We all used the same hymnal, same liturgy, same formats and expectations. It was all quite uniform.

Regardless of the situation—rural, suburban, city—the style and nature of worship across this denomination was static, similar, with only small variations.

In the twenty-first-century church that will not be so. From congregation to congregation, even within denominations, there will be considerable variety.

Most specifically, what a rural congregation may need in its worship life and ministry context can be quite divergent from what is needed in an urban environment or in the suburbs. And that's a better idea than the uniformity of my childhood.

Why should we all worship the same or practice our ministries in an identical manner? There are significant differences from location to location. And those differences need to be honored and appreciated.

Why should ethnic differences not count? In fact, we ought to emphasize the contribution of the lovely variety that different ethnic traditions can contribute to our worship experience.

And an ethnic appreciation goes way beyond just the hymns we sing or the language we speak. Full ethnic appreciation acknowledges sounds, looks, artistic differences, and even smells. The beautiful bouquet that is the human family ought to be lifted and celebrated. Make a real deal of our cultural contributions to the family of faith.

The key word is "contextual"—contextual—make it reflective of the context in which the ministry resides.

If it is a Latino community, then make it Latino. If it is African American, make it African American.

But also be sensitive to socioeconomic differences.

One congregation I served was very academic. The most frequent employer in the congregation was IBM. These were research and development engineers; well-educated folks. The second highest employer in the congregation was the local university—faculty and grad students. It was a very academically oriented culture. Therefore, my preaching style and the type of worship would be quite different than many other settings.

That's the kind of thing we mean by contextual.

It does not have to reflect some kind of denominational uniformity.

In fact, in the twenty-first-century church, denominationalism is also fading. For most twenty-first-century worshippers, they don't care what kind of denomination it is. What they care about is the quality of its spiritual nurture and the impact it is having on the life of those in the surrounding community. How is this congregation helping its members grow an ever deeper and richer relationship with the Holy? And what kind of difference is it making in the quality of life of those in its surrounding community? Those are the key questions.

We live in an "its-all-about-me" culture. "All you church people want is my time and my money. I don't have enough time, and I don't have enough money. So why should I get involved with your congregation? What difference are you making? Why is it worthy of my time and my money? Show me!"

By making it contextual, we are demonstrating that we honor the people who live in our environs and we want to connect with them in a legitimate way rather than trying to acculturate them to our style and traditions.

Acculturating just isn't working anymore. Again, as a child, I knew I needed to learn "how the church people do it so I could correctly do it their way"—even though it all seemed quite foreign to me. *Kyrie*—really? What's that?

Now we need to first immerse ourselves in the life of the community and let our worship and ministry organically rise out of that immersion. Be a part of the community in every way possible. Don't just exist in a neighborhood, but reflect and impact that neighborhood. Make it real. Make it connected. Make it contextual.

If we randomly stopped someone in the surrounding neighborhood and asked them what they know about our congregation, what would they say?

Most would say they know nothing about it. They have no connection. There's the rub.

We need to get out into the neighborhood. Make contacts. One approach to church growth teaches that we need to identify a community of about five hundred homes and then reach out and make at least seven contacts to each home in that community. Knock on the doors, hang door hangers, distribute fliers, do mailings, over and over again. Why seven times? Why do we see the same commercials on television over and over again? Because their marketing research has informed them that until we have seen that commercial at least eight times, we haven't gotten the message they want us to get. Repetition makes the point.

Even so in church growth. We need to repeatedly affirm for the community that we care about them. We want to journey with them as partners in the enrichment of their family's well-being. We want to invite them into our fellowship to enliven our fellowship with their impact—allowing them to change us.

After we have successfully approached those five hundred homes at least seven times, then move on to a new group of five hundred homes and start all over again.

Here's an example: I once supervised the start of a new Latino ministry in the South Side of Bethlehem, Pennsylvania. I asked the new mission developer not to hold a worship service for a full year. But during that year I asked him to walk the neighborhood, meet the people, build their trust, establish relationships, and build networks in the community. Then at the end of the year, when he finally began to hold worship he had a considerable number of people ready and eager to support the ministry because it grew organically from that networking, relationship building, and contextual respect.

That's what the twenty-first-century church is seeking. Make it contextual, not uniform. Make it reflect and honor the neighborhood in which it dwells. Make it grow from relationships with the community and networking across the neighborhood.

So what if it doesn't look like any other congregation in that denomination. Who cares?

Make it an alive and real response to the needs and character of the community and it will work.

Make it a vibrant and dynamic reflection of good news, hope, unconditional love and open future as those rightfully arise from the realities of the community.

Make it evident in action, not just in words.

Get out there and mingle, relate, network, and appreciate who they are and what touches their souls.

Contextual! Organic!

DISCUSSION

1. How well do we know the people who live in a two- to three-mile radius around our congregation? How can we get to know them better?

2. How can we better partner with our surrounding community to journey with them in their search for a healthier spiritual life?

3. What kind of changes will we need to make to be more contextual and less traditional? What resistance will we face? How can we address that resistance?

4. What outside resources will we need to become more contextual? Who will lead us in this effort?

Chapter Eight

From Didactic to Relationship

QUITE FRANKLY, WHAT IS important to the twenty-first-century church is not how many Bible verses you can memorize. It is not how well you memorized the Catechism. How well versed you may be in church history or even complex theology are not what impresses the twenty-first-century church.

Instead, they want to know what is the quality and depth of your relationship with God. That's the key.

My religious formation as a child growing up in the church was almost exclusively didactic. In Sunday School we learned *about* the Bible—its stories and contents. We learned some church history—especially the journeys of Saint Paul or the like.

And in confirmation we learned the Catechism. Did we *understand* the Lord's Prayer, the Ten Commandments, the creeds and the sacraments?

Further *education* involved *learning* right from wrong. We discussed moral and ethical decisions and approached that from a logical and rational argument.

We learned a lot *about* God and especially Jesus—but at no time was there any conversation about our *relationship* with God.

Even in seminary in the late 1960s, the curriculum was totally didactic. We studied the New Testament in ancient Greek. We had several classes on the Old Testament. We had multiple courses in systematic theology. We heard great lectures on church history. We learned an awful lot *about* the church with not one word about the quality or depth of our relationship to the Holy.

That was all appropriate in a *sola Scriptura* church. It made good sense that we became experts on the Bible. It was expected that we would then *teach* our parishioners what we had learned— pass on the *knowledge* from generation to generation without any regard for how deeply or qualitatively our members loved God.

And from the sixteenth century until the 1960s, it worked fairly well. The church thrived and did just fine.

However, in the congregation where I was confirmed, there was rampant racism, anti-Semitism, and other prejudices. We had some conversations about that, but no real association to our faith.

There was virtually no one challenging the cultural prejudices of our day. Oh, we heard about the evil of gambling or alcoholism or things like that. But no one dared to address the racism that was evident.

And there was very little attention to the needs of the poor, disenfranchised, forgotten, outcast, and isolated. We made token efforts at Christmas or once in a while, but no ongoing effort to engage in these real concerns.

The congregation reflected the culture and in a number of ways was an agent of the culture to transmit the culture—and all its prejudices—on to the next generations.

The culture and the church were seen as partners. The culture still affirmed the church. It was expected that everyone at least belonged to a congregation somewhere—even if they rarely attended.

In my teens, I know that every one of my close friends belonged to a church. They belonged to different mainline denominations, and some did not attend very often, but at least they held a membership.

Not so today. When I ask teenagers today if most of their friends are involved in a church somewhere, the answer is a resounding *no*! And to talk about one's faith among one's teenage friends would jeopardize one's popularity. It will not get you invited into the "in crowd." It may even get one isolated and marginalized. Not a good thing to do if one wants to be accepted and popular.

That's the nature of our culture today. Fifty percent of the children in kindergarten today in the United States are unchurched. For me, that's not acceptable. Yet there seems to be far too meager an effort to address that. It seems to be just accepted as "the way things are."

People lament the decline of the church, but are not concerned enough to do something about that.

The didactic approach is not stimulating or inspiring our members to be engaged with the culture on behalf of the faith.

Memorizing the Bible or the Catechism does not energize our members to be brave enough to share their faith with others.

I asked one congregation that I was serving if when they greeted each other when they gathered anytime at church that in addition to asking the usual "How are you?" questions—they would also asked, "How are you and God getting along with each other? What has been your faith struggle this past week?"

The very thought of that kind of personal exchange was terrifying to them. When I first suggested it, they laughed in response. "Come on, Pastor. You can't be serious. We don't do that here. That's not who we are."

"We don't do that here"—and 80 percent of our congregations are stagnant or dying!

Yes, it's not what we do here—but maybe it is exactly what we should be doing here?

Maybe we need to not be so intent on didactics—which are fine—please do not get me wrong.

Maybe instead of focusing all our efforts on *learning* the Bible or Catechism or the like . . .

Maybe instead we ought to focus primarily on our *relationship* with God and then use that hunger to have a richer and deeper relationship that can lead us to want to learn more about God, the Scriptures, and the church.

Without that quality of relationship, the passion behind the learning is shallow. Most of us never retained much of what we learned in Sunday School—if we ever really learned it at all.

Most of us never really integrated the teachings in our confirmation instruction in any life changing way.

Most of us seldom made the connection to the wonderful meaning of the sacraments and how we can live our lives.

For way too many of us, we could compartmentalize—church was church and daily life was daily life and seldom did the two integrate into each other.

What happened at church did not carry over to the rest of the week.

And I would propose it is because it lacked any emphasis on the *relationships* we can have with the Holy—that a Holy Father created us for a reason, a Savior died to defeat our death, and a Blessed Spirit empowers our lives to be vibrant agents of good news, hope, unconditional love and an open future.

The church is dying because we have not fostered genuine *relationships* with God and with the family of God.

What we need is to invest more energy in sharing "this is how it is for me . . ."

We need to be more intentional about discussing this sacred *relationship* and how it can impact all our days and our deeds.

We need to share with each other our spiritual struggles and our spiritual successes. And that needs to be a key part of our gathering every time we assemble at our congregations.

One suggestion: I like testimonials. I would love to see every congregation take just five minutes at least one Sunday a month during the worship service for lay people to give a personal testimony about how their relationship with God has made a real difference—in practical ways—in the way they live their lives.

True illustration: I served a congregation where one of our members was an honored, retired professor of theology from one of our seminaries. This respected and learned scholar would teach a Sunday School class once a month for the adult members. This was a fantastic opportunity to study at the feet of a highly regarded giant in our denomination.

At the same time, one Sunday a month, during the adult Sunday School class, a member would volunteer to discuss how they applied their faith in their career. For example, we have a member who was doing DNA research—almost literally playing "god." He discussed how he took his work seriously and did not minimize its impact.

The one that blew me away was a member who calculated the telephone rates we all paid for our telephone service. How can one apply one's faith in calculating telephone rates? Well he was sensitive to the fact that everyone needed to have a telephone in case of an emergency to be able to call 911. And he knew that the elderly on fixed incomes and the poor struggled to afford a telephone. So he convinced the phone company to have graduated telephone rates so that the elderly and the poor got their service at a cheaper rate, and the rest of us paid a little more so that the elderly and the poor could have telephones. Faith in action!

That's the kind of thing that needs to be more common in the midst of our faith communities and not at all exceptional.

What ways are we providing opportunities for that kind of holy conversation? How is it structured into the normal operations of our faith fellowship? How can we elevate such sharing as an expected part of our life together?

We need to respect the need to learn and to understand. Nothing wrong with that.

But that alone will not cut it anymore in the twenty-first-century church.

It's just not working. And we need to innovate and adapt to a church that is far more spiritual in its nature and in its activities.

How can we encourage our children to be in love with God?

How can we enable our adults to expand the depth and quality of their relationship with God?

We need to advance in that effort or the church will continue to decline.

DISCUSSION

1. To what extent has our congregation been more focused on knowing "about" Jesus rather than "knowing Jesus"—didactic versus relational?

2. How can we improve our efforts to enable all our members to develop an ever-deepening relationship with God—personal and heartfelt? Who will lead this effort?

3. How can we inform the surrounding community that our congregation is not a place that merely embraces a didactic approach but emphasizes a more relational approach to our faith? Who will lead this effort?

4. What resistance will we face by shifting from knowing "about" Jesus to truly and deeply "knowing Jesus"?

Chapter Nine

From Institution
to Movement

THE TWENTY-FIRST-CENTURY CHURCH DOES not want to be an institution. It wants to be a movement.

I looked up institution in the dictionary. The key concept to an institution is "established"—yes, established for a purpose, but also established as in laws, customs, constitutions, bylaws, traditions—one might say "stuck!"

I also looked up movement in the dictionary. A movement is something that is "moving"; "an organized group of people working toward or favoring a common goal."

Think of the civil rights movement—the women's movement—the environmental movement . . .

They were not burdened with a constitution or bylaws. They were not constrained by long-standing traditions—quite the opposite. They were not stuck doing the same old same old.

A movement is moving. It is alive with action and direction. It is dedicated to achieving a goal. It wants to make a real and tangible difference.

A movement is "don't tell me, show me" stuff.

This is a radical shift—perhaps the biggest change sought by the twenty-first-century church over *sola Scriptura*?

It is a dynamic expression of *sola Spiritus*. It means organizing like-minded people around a need for action expressed either locally or beyond that is motivated by the good news, hope, unconditional love and open future that the gospel inspires. It is people coming together to get results.

One of the main complaints from the twenty-first-century church is—"All you church people want is my time and my money. I don't have enough time and I don't have enough money. Why should I get involved? What difference are you making worthy of my community?"

What difference are we making worthy of commitment? That's a key question for the twenty-first-century church.

One question this begs is, how will we know what to do? What are the needs that beg for our action especially in our immediate communities.

I have a simple suggestion: *Ask them!*

I noted earlier how I asked a Latino pastor starting a new congregation to not hold a worship service until he had walked the neighborhood for a year, built a network of support, and gained the trust and confidence of the people. Only then was he ready to launch a new congregation.

The same for our existing congregations. How often are we out there, among the people who live in our surrounding neighborhoods, getting to know them, hearing their concerns, and organizing a meaningful response?

I mentioned the five hundred households that we approach at least seven times—this is a good beginning. Consistency is essential to demonstrate that we are more interested in them and the quality of their lives than in just putting "butts in our pews" so we can pay the bills.

Consistency testifies that we are "here for them"—inspired by the way our Lord is consistently here for us.

Consistency documents our willingness to do what needs to be done, to make the sacrifice and commitment to the cause as they see it—even as our Lord made the sacrifice and commitment for us.

We are up against it. Our reputations are not so hot. We have been too isolated from those who live around our congregations.

Oh, we welcome them for our pancake suppers or whatever. We are glad they show up for our fundraising activities. And if they muster the courage to actually try a worship service, we are generally welcoming.

But welcoming is no longer enough. We need to be *inviting*.

Historically, denominations like mine (Lutheran) grew two main ways: 1. Immigration (in the Lutheran case, from Northern Europe—the Germans, Scandinavians, etc.)—they came by the boat loads and established communities and built churches; 2. They had large families—my father was one of eight children, by mother was one of seven children. Big families mean big churches.

But now the boats stopped coming and someone invented "the pill" so that neither of those methods to grow congregations apply.

We need to do something else. We need to launch *movements* that will inspire people to join us in whatever cause we have identified to enhance the quality of life in our communities.

Get out there and engage in conversation with them and demonstrate our commitment and learn of their needs.

One way to do that is through a 501C3. A 501C3 is an IRS category for a nonprofit. Let me give an example.

I served an urban congregation that had a rising rate of juvenile delinquency in the neighborhood that logically concerned the residents. So we organized the West Hills Community Improvement Corporation (a 501C3).

On the board of directors of this corporation were three members from the congregation and eight members from the neighborhood so that it was more neighborhood driven and controlled than congregation.

The purpose of the 501C3 was to enhance the quality of life of the neighborhood and explicitly address the rise of juvenile delinquency. The stated purpose was not religious for a reason.

There are plenty of grants and funding for nonprofit organizations that are not religiously oriented. There are grants from the city, state, federal, and foundations all with the intent of supporting such efforts on community improvement without religious intentions (separation of church and state, etc.).

Through the West Hills Community Improvement Corporation we developed a vibrant community center in our church building. We had a state-licensed summer day camp that gave free breakfasts and lunches to the youth. We had after-school programs. The local Lutheran social ministry organization brought adult day care into our building. And we did it all at no cost to the congregation.

Yes, it took work—and there were documents like bylaws, etc. But the "institutional" part of it all did not overshadow the greater effort to connect with the youth of the neighborhood and make a difference.

There are resources to help:

- *Starting a Nonprofit at Your Church*, by Joy Skjegstad (Alban Institute, 2002)
- *Winning Grants to Strengthen Your Ministry*, also by Joy Skjegstad (Alban Institute, 2007)

We need not reinvent the wheel. There are resources to help us.

The key point I want to make is that staying stuck in our established institutions with all that encumbers us is just not working. Eighty percent of our congregations are stagnant or dying. The evidence is compelling. It's time to do something else.

Get out there and engage with the neighborhood. There are issues in every community.

I served in a financially prosperous community that one would assume had very few problems—certainly no presence of juvenile delinquent gangs. But instead there were issues with drugs and teen pregnancies.

I served in another wealthy community that had a very high divorce rate.

Wealth or financial stability does not eliminate problems.

And rural communities have plenty of their own issues as well.

Organize!

I live by a number of axioms—some are gleaned from other sources, some are my own.

One that I live by is—"Don't agonize, organize!"

Don't agonize over declining attendance and membership and increasing difficulty paying the bills—*organize!*

Get out there. Talk to people. Invite them into the church for "focus study groups" to hear their concerns and map out solutions.

Explore the 501C3 option. I have used it quite successfully in two different congregations and diverse situations.

Being a warm and welcoming congregation is no longer enough. We need to launch *movements* dedicated to paying forward the good news, hope, unconditional love and open future our God so graciously bestows upon us. To hoard it is a sin.

One of my favorite children's sermons that I do is to gather the children at the chancel and ask them what is their favorite flavor of ice cream—always gets a good response. I then share with them that my favorite is a Ben & Jerry's one, chunky monkey! Chunky monkey is banana ice cream with fudge chunks and walnuts—delicious! We pretend that we have an enormous bowl of our favorite ice cream—far more than we could eat ourselves. But there are children right there with us who have no ice cream at all. Would it be okay if we kept all the huge bowl of ice cream to ourselves and refused to share it with the other children who really want some of our ice cream? The children in the church resoundingly say, "No. That's selfish!" Well, we have an enormous supply of God's love, more than we will ever need ourselves. And there are children who know nothing about Jesus. Shouldn't we share? Shouldn't we tell them about Jesus so that they can know about how much God loves them too?

It's a good children's sermon.

How selfish are we with the good news, hope, unconditional love and open future that God so willingly gives to us? How delinquent are we with sharing that with others—even those in the neighborhoods right around our congregations?

The boats stopped coming—and someone invented "the pill." We are going to have to find other ways to grow our ministries.

Moving from institutions to movements is what the twenty-first-century church is desiring. Let's respond to their desires.

DISCUSSION

1. Institutions are often more focused on survival—paying the bills, maintaining the property—than in the mission of the organization. To what extent is our congregation an institution rather than a mission?

2. How can we more fully shift from institution to mission—genuinely putting the work of God's kingdom at the highest priority in partnership with the community? Who will lead this shift? What kind of resistance will we face? How will we address this resistance?

3. When we say we are a missional fellowship, do we know what that means? What would it look like? How can we get there?

4. What outside resources will we need to help us transition from a worshiping community that sometimes does mission to a missional community that worships? Who will manage this transition?

Chapter Ten

From Orthodoxy
to Orthopraxis

As I HAVE CONSISTENTLY been presenting, the twenty-first-century church is not impressed with all our words. Talk all we want, it does not move these predominantly younger adults—the *sola Spiritus* movement.

Sola Spiritus is all about being alive, dynamic, engaging, active, empowering, and brimming with hope and love. It *does* something, not just talk.

Orthodoxy means we get all the words right. We are "true to the faith" in all the correct ways. We articulate the faith properly and in keeping with the historic traditions of the church—the creeds, the Scriptures, the liturgies, etc.

Orthodoxy is not a bad thing. It is an accurate expression of what we believe. It is a right and true telling of what the church has taught for centuries. What could be wrong with that?

So the issue is not that orthodoxy is wrong. The issue is not to fight with the Scriptures. The issue is not to battle with the traditions.

The issue is—all those just don't work as they have done for so long.

So we can recite the creeds from memory . . .

So we can quote many chapters and verses from the Scriptures . . .

So we can do the liturgies without looking at the hymnal . . .

The twenty-first-century church would respond, "So what? What difference does it make?"

If it does not change people's lives . . .

If it does not impact the neighborhood constructively . . .

If it is not addressing the real issues in people's lives . . .

If it is not connected to the needs of the community . . .

If it is isolated and only impacts the members of the congregation . . .

If it does not reflect the problems that haunt those in need . . .

If it is all about us (crowd religion) and does not demonstrate a real commitment to the faith (discipleship) . . .

If it does not make it safe for us to be honest about our faults and failures (transition/transformation) . . .

If it does not inspire the faithful to fully surrender in trust to the movement of the Holy Spirit (life in the Spirit) . . .

If it merely repeats all the old stuff the church has been doing that is just no longer working . . .

If it does not afford a solid argument why anyone should commit their time, talent and energy when all those are in short supply . . .

If it does not demonstrate a compelling narrative around which we can organize our lives . . .

Then why bother? Why bother?

That's a fundamental position of the twenty-first-century church.

Give me a reason to get involved. And all those old excuses based on guilt or whatever won't work. Don't even try.

Instead, portray—in action—a compelling narrative that demonstrates an unreserved dedication to the good news, hope, unconditional love and an open future.

Do it—in visible ways—that can serve as a role model that expresses the labors of the faithful.

Don't tell me—*show me!*

And that's a huge challenge for most of our congregations.

Too much of what our congregations do exists only within their walls or among their members.

Too much is for the benefit of "the club" and not for those outside "the club."

Too much reflects the awful expression, "Charity begins at home . . ." which I believe has little to do with the teachings of Jesus.

Too much energy and resources are consumed by "the club" with the small, remaining tidbits given to those outside "the club."

I heard one church-growth expert say that in growing congregations, the pastor spends more than half her/his time outside the congregation—out in the community, connecting with the community, and responding to the needs of the community.

This is possibly the most critical aspect if we are going to be seen as worth the effort by the twenty-first-century church.

This, maybe more than anything else, will be the litmus test for the twenty-first-century church to measure whether or not they want to be involved.

Are we making a difference?

Are we doing something that impacts more than ourselves?

Are we willing to make the sacrifices—the hard work—to make it happen?

Are we willing to be measured more by our actions than our words?

Maybe we should be thinking in terms of "visible sermons"—faith active in love—more than all the eloquent elucidations we pontificate from our pulpits?

Maybe we should emphasize effort to strategize engagements with the neighborhoods instead of memorizing Scripture?

Maybe we should worry whether we are "proclaiming the gospel at all times, and when necessary using words" (attributed to Saint Francis)?

The twenty-first-century church is not impressed with our words—it is deeds that will win the day.

From orthodoxy to orthopraxis . . .

DISCUSSION

1. To what extent have we been focused on getting our teaching and preaching correct instead of getting our actions faithful and correct?

2. What will we need to do to shift from a predominately "orthodoxy" model to a predominately "orthopraxis" model? Who will lead that transition?

3. What would an orthopraxis congregation look like? How do we get there?

4. What outside resources will we need to assist us in this transition? Who will be responsible to engage those outside resources?

Chapter Eleven

Implementation

NOW THAT WE HAVE discussed a great deal of the "what" of the twenty-first-century church, let's focus on the how. How are we going to implement all these changes?

I have served in five interim pastor positions with congregations in various stages of crisis that needed to make some serious changes. Here is a process that I have used with repeated success.

1. Organization: I would convene a transition team of no more than twelve members—people who are both well respected in the congregation but also progressive in their approach. You will need people who are trusted and also open and honest—people who value transparency and will be forward thinking. This transition team will be accountable to the governing board of the congregation and will work as the management group for the transitional process.

2. Education: I hold a series of adult classes to educate the members on the twenty-first-century church and all its demands. We also explore things like conflict management and power utilization which often become key elements in systemic change. I average about eight sessions in this program, enough to present the key material. Given the ten chapters prior to his one, I would suggest ten educational sessions, one for each chapter in this book.

3. Cottage Meetings: to assist the congregation in the journey to making sound decisions about its future, I have held a series of what I call cottage meetings (or small group meetings) of no more than fifteen people at any meeting—so you can calculate how many meetings you will need for your congregation. The meetings are as follows:

- Where have we been: looking at the history (the last ten years or so) of the congregation with questions like:

  › What have been the best times in this congregation?
  › What made them so good?
  › What were the difficult times?
  › What made them so difficult?
  › What can we learn from the good times?
  › What can we learn from the difficult times?
  › What does that tell us as we look forward?

  (Notice I focus on the *what* and never the *who*. It isn't who did wrong, but what went wrong. We can change the what—the who we cannot always change.)

- Where are we now? I use some questions noted below and I also take this opportunity to present the grid from chapter 1 and review, again, the various aspects and emphases of the twenty-first-century church:

  › What are we doing now that is really working?
  › What makes it so successful?
  › What are we doing now that isn't so successful?
  › What keeps it from being successful?
  › What can we learn from our successes?
  › What can we learn from those efforts that were not successful?

> › What about the new issues with the twenty-first-century church?

> › What do we need to change to be open to the twenty-first-century church?

(Again, it is the *what*, not the *who!*)

- Where is God calling us to be? Here is a chance to pull together some learnings from the first two cottage meetings with an eye to some movement toward the twenty-first-century church. With questions like:

> › What is God calling us to change in order to keep God's church alive and vital in the twenty-first century?

> › Which of those changes can we make more easily?

> › Which of those changes will require greater effort?

> › Does everyone need to make the same changes? Can there be options? Can we, for now, be both *sola Scriptura* and *sola Spiritus*?

> › How can we continue to make a welcoming place for the *sola Scriptura* people while we also make a welcoming place for the *sola Spiritus* people?

> › What are the next steps we need to take?

In this way we are inviting the entire congregation to have a stake in the future of the ministry without "taking sides." For now, *sola Scriptura* people are not wrong, it is just that we are on the edge of a new beginning, a new era in the evolution of God's church.

We can not linger in the *sola Scriptura* era—I believe that is one key reason why 80 percent of our churches are stagnant or dying.

And not everyone is ready for the *sola Spiritus* age that is unfolding.

Where possible, can we, for now, accommodate both? For example: one worship service in the *sola Scriptura* style, rich in tradition—and one worship service in the *sola Spiritus* style, designed around the experiential.

In making systemic changes, changes that impact the entire ministry, it is critical to have broad "ownership." By using the cottage meeting model, we invite everyone to have a say and be included in the process.

4. Inspiration: I would take the opportunity to emphasize God's calling to a new and exciting future in the worship through both sermons and prayers. I would emphasize how God has always led God's people through good times and bad to the future God desires for them. Now it is our opportunity to embrace the journey, accept the adventure, and be faithful to the challenge of becoming a twenty-first-century church. Probably not in every sermon, but at least monthly I would make some reference to this sacred adventure.

Our challenge is huge. I can summarize it like this:

- We need to move from being a worshipping fellowship that sometimes does mission

- To a missional fellowship that worships.

What I mean by that is that currently we are essentially worshipping fellowships gathered around Word and Sacraments, which sometimes dedicates some of our efforts on mission for others.

A mission fellowship is centered on that outreach to others—that *orthopraxis*—that living demonstration of the good news, hope, unconditional love and open future that the gospel uniquely gives us. It is dynamic and visible. It is the reason for the congregation's being. We gather for the primary purpose to *do something with others*. Notice, *with*, not *for*. That is a huge difference.

Just think: "Here, let me do this *for* you . . ." *or* "Come, let us do this *together* . . ." Missional fellowships seek to *partner* with others to get things done in a respectful and dignified and relevant way.

Worship for the missional fellowship is essential. Worship, Word and Sacrament, give us our nurture, our values, our inspiration and the empowerment to launch into the adventure. Without Worship, Word and Sacrament, we will be weak and adrift. Worship is not the reason we exist—but it is essential for our healthy life together.

5. Vocabulary: We cannot change something as large and as complex as a system—a congregation—without changing its vocabulary. As long as we continue to use the same language, we are stuck in the same systemic way of doing things. If what we seek is a new way—a twenty-first-century way—we will need to adopt the new vocabulary of that era. Some language does carry over—I would strongly suggest: good news, hope, unconditional love, and an open future—but now infused with new and more dynamic meaning. No longer just words—these now come alive with actions, experiences, results. New vocabulary denotes a new way of being with each other and our surrounding communities. It invites us to think like a missional fellowship that partners with those outside the congregation to truly make a difference. It is different and requires new ways of speaking.

6. Ready-Fire-Aim: The church has for too long been locked in the "Ready-Aim-Fire" mentality that mandates that we don't do something (*fire*) until we are *ready* and have carefully *aimed*. The net result is that too often it looks like "Ready-Aim-Aim-Aim-Aim . . ." and we seldom if ever get to "Fire." The adventure to moving into a new way of being with no guarantee of success will require us to adopt a "Ready-Fire-Aim" attitude. Give it a try. See what happens. Give yourselves permission to fail. Often we learn more from our failures than from our successes. Then try and try again. So ultimately it looks like "Ready-Fire-Aim-Fire-Aim-Fire-Aim," etc. Always trying and always learning and developing.

7. Judicatory: I am a pastor in the Delaware-Maryand Synod of the Evangelical Lutheran Church in America. I have a bishop and a whole system of accountability. That is both a blessing and a curse. When the system and the bishop are aware of this unfolding twenty-first-century church and are supportive of pastors and congregations that are struggling to be open and responsive to this new era in God's church, that is good (as my bishop is). But if there is not support and encouragement from that judicatory level, then it is more challenging. Beyond support and encouragement, I would ask those judicatory systems to be advocates for the changes that the twenty-first-century church is calling us to make. These are fundamental and penetrating changes that can be upsetting. It is not easy to let go of the traditional ways that have existed for these last five hundred years. And the path to this twenty-first-century church is not yet fully clear. We know some of the characteristics, but have no assurance of the way to achieve success. I have presented ways that I have used with success and encourage us all to be inventive. Being inventive when the members of the congregation want to be traditional means taking some risks. If we use the methods described in this chapter, we minimize the resistance by building from the bottom up, by ensuring investment and broad ownership of the process and the results from across the membership. But there will always be pockets of resistance. In the face of that resistance, support from the judicatory is needed. That support ought to be represented in workshops and educational and inspirational events sponsored by the judicatory to address the various aspects of the twenty-first-century church and how we can best respond. Best practices, attempts, and learnings can be shared and a collegial approach adopted. There is no need to be alone in this journey. It will go far better when we journey together, learn from each other's attempts, celebrate each other's successes, comfort each other in the face of attempts that did not go so well, and in general truly be one family in God's church gathered for mission in

various locations. Let's band together in deeper and more precious ways to encourage and support each other.

There is an African proverb: If you want to go fast, go alone. If you want to go far, go together. We don't need fast. We need far.

Let me close with a poem that inspires me. It depicts this journey from the old to the new—with the blessing and active support of those who have gone on before us and are now reaching out to those who are just now coming along the way.

The poem is "The Bridge Builder," by Will Allen Dromgoole:

> An old man traveling a lone highway,
> Came at the evening cold and gray,
> To a chasm vast and deep and wide,
> Through which was flowing a sullen tide.
> The old man crossed in the twilight dim,
> The sullen stream held no fears for him.
> But he turned when safe on the other side,
> And built a bridge to span the tide.
> "Old man," cried a fellow pilgrim near,
> "You're wasting your time in building here,
> Your journey will end with the close of day,
> You never again will pass this way,
> You've crossed the chasm deep and wide,
> Why build you this bridge at eventide?"
> The builder lifted his old grey head,
> "Good friend, in the path I have come," he said,
> "There followeth after me today,
> A youth whose feet must pass this way.
> This stream which has been as naught to me,
> To that fair haired youth may pitfall be,
> He, too, must cross in the twilight dim.
> Good friend, I'm building this bridge for him."

Jesus, at enormous expense, built a bridge for us called Salvation. Now it is our turn—to make the sacrifice—to let go of the past—to embrace a new and exciting future—to embark on a sacred journey—to attempt what we've never done before—inspired by God's good news, hope, unconditional love and open future—to join in the movement that is the new, twenty-first-century church!

DISCUSSION

1. Are we ready and willing to become a twenty-first-century church? If so, to what extent? If not, why not? How will we address this?

2. What are the next steps to become a twenty-first-century church? Who will manage this process? What kind of resistance will we encounter? How will we address this resistance?

3. Those leading this powerful transition will need a lot of support. What will we put in place to support and encourage those assigned with the task of leading our congregation in this transition?

4. When will we start?!

CPSIA information can be obtained
at www.ICGtesting.com
Printed in the USA
LVHW080416210622
721754LV00014B/269